EASY MANAGING GUIDE

FOR MODERN MANAGERS & EMPLOYEES

VIJAYKUMAR GUMMADI

ISBN 979-888546432-1

To my wife

Swapna Gummadi

Contents

Contents

Contents

Foreword

Modern complexities in all areas of organization making Managers and Employees unprepared for tomorrow.

Being Process Engineering Professional and Nuclear Expert enabled me to know Latest International Management Techniques.

This book "EASY MANAGING GUIDE For Modern Managers & Employees"concentrates on many important areas of skill and knowledge that contributes to executing tasks in different areas of managing modern organization.

You may find these 825 easy & immensely practical tips and sound advice with commonsense under seventy five managing aspects of organization very interesting that you don't find elsewhere.

This book is helpful for busy tomorrows Managers and Employees of all types of organizations.

VIJAYKUMAR GUMMADI

CHAPTER ONE

ABILITY/ TALENT

1)Hard work is the answer to everything. If you want to become like a sun first you need burn like a sun.

2)If you are talented hard work will be opportunity for exhibiting and if you are lack of talent, hard work will compensate your inadequacies.

3)People with real strengths are rare like finding a treasure. When you can do common things in most uncommon ways that is your talent. Talent makes world to talk.

4)Appreciated effort but not the talent.

5)Naturally acquired abilities leads us to glory.

6)To become best version of yourself requires unlearning also.

7)Nothing impossible for a skill with diligence.

8)People should sophisticated enough to make competent use of technical knowledge.

9)Leaders should possess ability to discover ability in others.

10)Everybody has talent but only few possess courage to use talent everywhere.

11)Development training programs expand peoples capabilities beyond the expected functional skill to action skills.

CHAPTER TWO

ACHIEVEMENT

1)Main road block for achievement is staying persistently focused on your goals in an environment of distractions. Real test for achievement is how much sustained is your persistence.

2)Mind is a fountain of thoughts. Hence try to be rational, just ignore distractions. Unless you possess clarity, your plan can't be a reality.

3)You can achieve your goals when you are honest to yourself. Right attitude for achievement is more important than any other attribute. Unless you have achieved 50% of your goal you can't consider your efforts as part of progress for achievement.

4)Establish culture of trust to gain individual commitment to achievement. Ensure everybody's involvement to your commitment.

5)Rely on your true strengths not on weaknesses. Mentor to enhance performance. Don't be aimless, know what you want, you can't achieve unless you know it.

6)Priorities are more important for strategy implementation. Continuous and continual progress review is mandatory for all important activities. Regular introspection is required to achieve anything substantial.

7)Unrealistic performance goals can trigger cascading irreversible consequences. Be open & true with all w.r.t. objectives, delays and difficulties.

8)Resort to risk only if chances for success are high. When things go wrong, look for solutions not for scape goats. Sudden flights never take you to any achievement.

9)If your thoughts are in right direction, you are on right course. Behavioral consequences are more profound and far reaching than managerial decisions. Pessimistic people do see problems in every situation.

10)Independence can be satisfying to individuals, but can also be threatening to all others, hence regulators & regulations are must.

11)When a plan doesn't work, change the plan but not the goal. Anything is possible if you have right people to support you at right time and at right place.

CHAPTER THREE

ACTION

1)Inaction is a character of a imperfect person.

2)Never resort to any action under indecisiveness or doubt.

3)Action is a reflection of your heart.

4)A good decision perpetually postponed is only a negative action.

5)Good nature and good heart must come together for good action.

6)Actions alone trustable. Your actions speaks your future.

7)Inaction is a misleading direction. Inaction is comparatively expensive than mistake. You can overcome difficulties only by actions.

8)Action is a footprint. Your actions proves who you are. Initiation in more important. Action dissolves doubt.

9)Never commit to what you can't do. Action is true character made visible.

10)Action is a bridge between your dreams and your reality. Action is a resultant of inner you and outer you.

11)Action lays foundation for achievement. Powerful actions will come from powerful intent.

CHAPTER FOUR

AGE

1)Nature gives you beautiful face but it is upto individuals how to appear as they age.

2)We are newer every day but not by age.

3)Age never handicap you but it is how you use.

4)Feelings are reflections of your true age.

5)Children are pure Aged tends to reflect children.

6)When you are unconscious of your age you live better.

7)Growing up and getting aged are not the same.

8)Age is associated with mindset.

9)Understanding comes with aging.

10)Psychologically age imposes limitations on your dreams.

11)Your attitude is more important than your age. Curiosity and enthusiasm outlives the age.

CHAPTER FIVE

ANGER

1)Anger creates delusion. Anger and intolerance are twins. Fruit if anger is a bad consequences.

2)Your anger is a cruel punishment you give it to self.

3)You can't see your true world when you are anger.

4)Angry persons are emotionally stupid. Anger generates destructive emotions.

5)There is a prevailing dormant pain underneath an anger. Anger is a reaction to pain.

6)Anger is a triggered protection of personality. Angry person will becomes emotionally stupid.

7)When you are calm people don't know where and what to attack, because there is known indication.

8)Refrain from action and speech when you're angry. Anger is sign of weakness.

9)Constructive anger can become a catalyst for change.

10)People who are capable of making you anger are controlling you. You loose your conscience when angry.

11)Controlling emotions of anger and frustrations is crucial for progress and achievement in life.

CHAPTER SIX

CHANGE

1)Change is the law of human existence. Change is unavoidable. Nothing is static except change.

2)Without change there is neither growth nor progress.

3)Everything what perceive is a dynamic instant of change.

4)Nothing can resist change, ultimately everything has to succumb to change. If you resist change you will be a victim.

5)Handling change is called experience. Wisdom is mastering change.

6)Those who continuously change as per circumstances can only survive.

7)If you don't know fact that change is only transitional, change will become a problem to you.

8)Change follows problems. Change begins with questioning.

9)To enable change, concentrate on few that really count. Inform about adverse side effects of change.

10)There is a hidden opportunity awaiting with every change.

11)Good things or bad things they exists for moment like snapshot.

CHAPTER SEVEN

CHARACTER

1)Character builds gradually.

2)Self image springs out of character.

3)Your personality creates your character.

4)Character is formed by life experiences.

5)Most people pretend to possess moral character though not.

6)Character is habits formed by engraved experiences.

7)Unconscious tendency of personality is character.

8)Good character adds to beauty of personality.

9)Character is how you look inside.

10)Good character undermines volatile emotions and enables balanced actions.

11)Character is how you treat those who can do nothing for you.

CHAPTER EIGHT

CONFIDENCE

1)Dependence on others makes you lose self confidence. Confidence is gained either by experience or by on job training.

2)Don't get caught up is a pessimistic loop of negative thinking. Anxiety is a cause of loosing self confidence. Training helps overcome anxiety. Making one comfortable to their surroundings reduces anxiety.

3)Never doubt, believe in your ability. Always maintain positive attitude.

4)Appreciate yourself and credit what you deserve. Never carve for approval of others.

5)Having mentor is a good idea that boosts confidence.

6)Being with your strengths makes you confident.

7)If you have confidence in yourself, others also believe you.

8)What you think of you is more important than what others think of you.

9)Confidence is a feeling of assurance you give to others as opportunities unfold in front of you.

10)Self confidence is prerequisite for any achievement. Confidence generates assurance. Your confidence creates your future.

11)When you don't compare with others it is a reflection of your confidence.

CHAPTER NINE

CONFLICT

1)Conflict are common, unavoidable and not preventable.

2)Most find skewed solutions for conflicts, momentarily forgetting their goals for a while.

3)Conflict is not good versus bad, but it is one man's beliefs versus another man's beliefs.

4)Conflict is a war inside you & and is battle of himself. You can never win a conflict by onside force.

5)Peace is ability to manage conflict but not escaping from conflict. Love all including our enemies, however whomsoever we fight we must protect our own interests.

6)Conflicts are built-up due to avoidance and autocratic thinking. Caution, some are interested to keep conflicts alive just to create history.

7)Root cause of most of the Conflicts lies in our fundamental assumptions of the issue. You can't understand conflicts when your heart is unopened.

8)Conflicts avoidance disconnects us and indirectly affects productivity. Avoidance of conflict further aggravates the issue.

9)Real conflict is in-between your heart and mind. Honest conversations could fix many conflicts. One can't work with two interests simultaneously. When your heart wins over your mind you won the Conflict.

10)Escalation of Conflict increases your ignorance, that makes you isolated from reality and truth. Conflict is a difference between your history and your plans.

11)Biased solutions for conflicts drifts your plan from main course permanently, making you never able to achieve your goals. Resolution of conflicts for mutual benefit enables trust and reliability.

CHAPTER TEN

CONSCIENCE

1)Conscience is original man inside you. Conscience is authentic.

2)Conscience is a light house for your inner self. Conscience is a internal thinking.

3)You are more afraid of your heart than anything else.

4)He is brave who obeys his conscience.

5)Conscience is only way to glory.

6)Mistakes are common but continuing in mistake is a blunder not accepting conscience.

7)Conscience contradicts majority consensus.

8)Conscience is pure, radiating and untouchable.

9)Mind overpowers conscience of individual.

10)Human will become animals without conscience.

11)Your conscience is a constant reminder of your ethics and values.

CHAPTER ELEVEN

COMMUNICATION

1)Communication is two way. One way is called information.

2)Unrestricted flow of information and communication across organization Structure critical for achievement of goals.

3)Only share information to those who need to know.

4)Intentional partial(part) communication is dangerous than no communication as it misleading.

5)Keep your communication as simple as possible.

6)We try to reply rather trying to understand communication i.e. communication gap.

7)Empathy is required for communication.

8)Those who dislike will broadcast your failures not your success.

9)Good communication is understanding what he misunderstands others.

10)Good communication results in immediate persuasion by others.

11)Incommunicable minds are root cause for triggered conflicts or controversies.

CHAPTER TWELVE

CONTROL

1)What exhausts your mind controls your life. What you allow will continue to control your life.

2)When you can't control; At least control the affect of consequences, if not, what you can't control will control us back.

3)Don't allow selfish people to control your life those who did little to your life.

4)Your relationships will be good as long as you control your emotions. Distinguish between those who care and control.

5)People could never control their emotions; they do not know what not to speak.

6)Power without a control corrupts. Only be concerned about what you can control.

7)Your personality is beautiful when your attitude is under control.

8)You got two options either control your life or be controlled in life. What you can't control must be endured.

9)What you are trying to hide, controls your life.

10)When you can't control your time you can't control your life.

11)When nothing is under your control just relax don't get stressed for no reason.

CHAPTER THIRTEEN

COST

1)List out 20% of activities that cost 80% of the total cost and focus, concentrate on them to reduced cost of them due to slippage.

2)Periodically follow zero budgeting and discard tasks becoming meaningless due to changed unanticipated circumstances.

3)Make provisions for uncertainties.

4)Seek accountability for assigned financial responsibilities.

5)Never approve escalations without reasonable reasons and justification.

6)All financial deviations must be approved two steps above.

7)Align financial progress with construction progress to move in tandem.

8)Follow financial control budgets and monitor financial progress continuously.

9)Adopt just in time inventory management.

10)Punish and penalize for deliberate financial misbehaviour.

11)Have regular financial audits and improve financial system shortfalls.

CHAPTER FOURTEEN

COURAGE

1)Most people who speak brave are not the one who do.

2)Uncertainty can't be managed without courage.

3)Progress can happen only with courage.

4)Courage undermines negativity.

5)Courage is love for your goal.

6)Courage is a definer of outcomes at turning points.

7)Courage is generated within.

8)Sometimes courage can overtake controls.

9)Courage is your decision.

10)Courage is your determination to act under unfavourable and uncertain circumstances.

11)Courage is antidote for fear.

CHAPTER FIFTEEN

CREATIVITY

1)To think creative you need to bypass your assumptions.

2)Question the accepted to look in a new way. Ask even ridiculous questions. Never accept ideas without questioning them.

3)Remove self imposed mental roadblocks.

4)Nature's examples are the best creativity ever.

5)Invest in time in learning to think differently.

6)Randomness is a beautiful tool for creativity.

7)Break natural barrier of mind.

8)Creative mind is a mind of child.

9)Self doubt is a enemy of creativity.

10)Creativity is something which will inspire others.

11)Challenge barriers of disbelief.

CHAPTER SIXTEEN

CULTURE

1)Act swiftly on tumours. Listen to unhappy employees. Coaching is an effective means of changing your current behaviour.

2)Cultivate relationships eliminate immediately relationship problems of team. No individual in organisation is completely independent.

3)You are prevented being optimistic when you are surrounded by pessimistic culture. Organisation lies in hearts and souls of its personnel.

4)Culture is a medium in-between personnel's actions and intentions. You cannot implement a strategic strategy in a bad culture.

5)Culture is not born and it is created. Practiced values depends upon prevailing culture. Culture shapes values.

6)Culture is a way of life. Culture is a frame of organization. Culture creates unspoken brand image. When culture don't exists anarchy dominates. Culture alone guarantees future.

7)Culture compensates for differences in diversity. Multiple cultural exposures fosters your growth. Culture expands your mind.

8)Right in principle should be best loved for creating better organization culture. Pure individuals with noble thoughts and deeds can only help organisations lead forward not the finance alone.

9)Without nourishing culture of organization, development of individual personality is unthinkable. Progressive culture prevails when every man judge by himself by what he has himself read.

10)Political passion cannot be allowed to go to such lengths effecting tolerance and freedom of thought.

11)Respect for every honest opinion prevails in a thriving culture. Men like that are needed to build up a healthy culture.

CHAPTER SEVENTEEN

DECISION

1)Generate large number of ideas before reaching a decision.

2)Provide adequate time for arriving critical decisions. Encourage full participation.

3)Evaluate and judge alternatives before arriving at a decision. Involve only positive people.

4)Implement easiest ideas initially. Never implement ideas unless you truly understand what they truly represent.

5)Keep reviewing and questioning till you are satisfied with ideas. Listen to the objections of important persons.

6)Action on good decisions is more important than arriving at good decision.

7)More the alternatives more difficulty in decision making.

8)Flaws in judgement occur due to prejudice and lack of empathy.

9)Our decisions are based on what makes sense to us. Delay is worst form of denial.

10)Never make permanent decisions on temporary feelings.

11)If you make rules you need not make decisions.

CHAPTER EIGHTEEN

DISCIPLINE

1)Discipline indirectly indicates trust.

2)Absence of discipline is the cause of many problems.

3)Discipline is creating order.

4)Discipline enables focus and being objective.

5)You can ignore distracting thoughtsbvwhen you are disciplined.

6)Discipline is the link between your goals and accomplishments.

7)Discipline keeps you doing for achieving goals like a habit.

8)Discipline work for objective rather for self needs.

9)Discipline enables to achieve long-term goals.

10)Most of the time discipline proves better than motivation or talent.

11)Discipline is essential for learning.

CHAPTER NINETEEN

EDUCATION

1)Teaching alone cannot render fundamental principles of life.

2)Education should help a young person to grownup in a good spirit.

3)More we educate ourselves less we tend to have commonsense.

4)Being trustable opens window of volunteering helping hand of others for further educating us.

5)No body can teach somebody something, unless engaged, unless essence of education is not felt.

6)Real education always keeps you productive. Good education teaches too less useless things.

7)Learning and understanding are different. Education may not inculcate understanding ability.

8)Educated and intelligent persons will always bring facts forefront. True education gives ability to think straight.

9)Education is not a title, it's a continuous process. Matured education imparts way to learn.

10)Peak of education is wisdom. Education gives ability to distinguish between good and evil.

11)Imagination triggers ideas but ideas are not experience. Experienced only shall teach.

CHAPTER TWENTY

EGO

1)Ego kills your relationships, your talents and your growth. You can't meet your highest self with ego.

2)Ego develops when you live in separation with others.

3)Avoid those who defend their ego and offend your soul.

4)Trust is inversely proportional to ego.

5)Your ego prevents you from becoming greatest or successful. Ego beyond threshold kills your talent.

6)Ego is what he was. Egoist is someone telling about themselves that you are forced to listen without judgement. Ego denies others reality.

7)More the knowledge you acquire less the ego you possess.

8)Your imprisoned cage is your ego. Ego is your illusion of yourself.

9)Ego makes you feel nothing is more important than you. Ego is one sort of self created elevated threshold yourself respect.

10)Love and friendship can only melt ego. In ego versus love, most of the time ego dominates.

11)Egoist as a leader if unchecked can sink a ship of whole team. Egoism is a self tranquilizer that makes you insensitive to others feelings.

CHAPTER TWENTY-ONE

EMOTIONS

1)If you have heart, there is a room for everything.

2)Make best impression on heart of your personnel.

3)Encourage informal gathering of personnel for bondage.

4)You can't just ignore emotions of your personnel.

5)Simple human touch enables to be more productive with least effort.

6)Help people with behaviour problems with counselling.

7)If you surrender to emotions of others you can never be productive. Emotions are impulsive.

8)Unaddressed emotions can seed stress and unhappiness.

9)Memory of emotional experience is prolonged.

10)Your emotions are you, reflections of you. Main reason for most of human actions is emotion.

11)You can quench others emotions just by making them to understand.

CHAPTER TWENTY-TWO

EQUALITY

1)It is called equality when you give same treatment to similar persons.

2)Equality in reality is very by rare.

3)Truth prevails only when all similar persons are treated equal.

4)Clandestine dissent is seeded by inequality.

5)Acceptance of unequal favour is injustice.

6)Equality is only theoretical.

7)Racism can be a reason for cascading inequality. Tolerating racism is racism.

8)Common good can't be realised in inequality.

9)Equality is a real democracy.

10)Laws, rules, regulations, governance, management exists only to enforce equality and to prevent discrimination.

11)Equality spreads love among and bonds people.

CHAPTER TWENTY-THREE

EXCELLENCE

1)You are the excellent when you realise your full abilities and potentials, though you may not be at par with the requirement.

2)Continuously and continually improve self to be excellent.

3)Remember, non can perfectly match the requirement, you have to only develop on task.

4)Be relentless in improving in leisure time.

5)You may be good however you have to be excellent.

6)If you are wise you will never aim impossible objectives.

7)We become our best by criticism of others.

8)Excellence is a glittering shine, which few seek where as others try to hide by it's shadow.

9)Excellence is a process. Excellence is doing your best and making impact.

10)When you are at your full potential amazing things will happen.

11)Excellence is professional art.

CHAPTER TWENTY-FOUR

EXPERIENCE

1)Knowledge can be gained only through personal experience.

2)Experience is an emotional memory.

3)Experience is only gained with non routines and uncertainties.

4)Experience can gained only by actually learning to sail ship through storms.

5)Experience destroys seeds of creativity.

6)Your reaction is a reflection of your experience.

7)Experience is a deep insight of possibilities.

8)When your are with your heart your are inexperienced and when you are with your mind you are experienced.

9)Experience is a felt truth.

10)Experienced never errs.

11)Experience can be acquired by onjob induction training.

CHAPTER TWENTY-FIVE

FAILURE

1)Failure is delayed achievement not a defeat. Failure is a detour. Fear of failure is major cause of failures.

2)We can never prevent probability of failures, however we can minimise effect of failure consequences.

3)Failure is due to doing things not exactly right. Failure is inability to practice practically one's own experience.

4)Failure is inevitable when you try to please everyone. When you try to convince everyone it's a compromise for failure.

5)People think more of what others think of their failures rather about their failure. You can learn consequences of failure only when you accept failures.

6)Failure is not a mistake. Failure is ones throttled optimal performance limited by circumstances.

7)If you avoid failure you will also avoid success, because road is same.

8)Failure is beginning afresh. Failure is a part of success. Failure builds strong character.

9)Only difference between success and failure is ability. Failure is a reality when you stop trying.

10)Failure is a leadership confusion in deciding what is important to all. Most people are preoccupied with insignificant thinking.

11)Excuses are foundation stone for a house of failures. Excuses never achieved anything great.

CHAPTER TWENTY-SIX

FAITH

1)Faith is a force of existence.

2)Blindly one can walk by faith.

3)Faith can only see what it believes.

4)Faith will guide you.

5)Extent of love for your goal alone can create faith for achieving.

6)People with faith can do miracles.

7)Faith delivers more than plans.

8)Faith is an extraordinary insight with a very powerful feeling for achieving.

9)Faith do not eliminate exists questions.

10)If you have faith you get everything.

11)Faith believes what you can't see.

CHAPTER TWENTY-SEVEN

FEAR

1)Don't decide your future out of fear. Look beyond fear, you will find your alternatives for a solution.

2)Fear is created out of ignorance. You fear melts away when you try to understand.

3)Fear of unknown is the main reason for procrastination.

4)You start growing the moment you have overcome your fear.

5)Fear creates illusion, magnifies things and stops life. Fear limits us.

6)Most people are defeated by their fears rather by competition.

7)What you really wanted is there beyond your fear. Hence you must confort your fear.

8)You can overcome your fears when you are master of your mind but not when mind mastered you.

9)Working with ethics & integrity leaves no room for fear.

10)Your suffering is proportional to your fear but not to the reality.

11)Fear is expensive than failure. It's a good teacher.

CHAPTER TWENTY-EIGHT

FLEXIBILITY

1)Undisciplined mind is better adaptable. Flexible are emphatic.

2)Flexible never gets out of shape.

3)Stay focused on your goals with flexible approach.

4)Flexibility enables self-awareness and triggers growth.

5)Flexible survives even in harsh conditions. Problems are no more problems for flexible.

6)Flexible are pioneers of change.

7)Your intelligence is your adaptability.

8)Those who don't change with time, they are changed.

9)Good education makes you adaptable. Being adaptable keeps your foot on ground.

10)Strength comes by your adaptability and flexibility. Life is learning to dance upto the rain.

11)Adaptability quotient is more important than Intelligence quotient and emotional quotient.

CHAPTER TWENTY-NINE

FREEDOM

1)Freedom is a liberty granted to conscience.

2)Unchecked freedom can be expensive.

3)Boundaries must be set for freedom.

4)Modest freedom is essential for Productivity.

5)Freedom enables opportunity for value addition in work.

6)Self discipline gives you required freedom.

7)Freedom gives you opportunity to do what you like.

8)Freedom is granted to make you and others better.

9)Freedom is your reaction to your circumstances.

10)Freedom is freedom from what others think.

11)Freedom is not free.

CHAPTER THIRTY

GENIUS

1)Genius makes things happen.

2)Genius is as curious as child.

3)Genius knows only perspiration.

4)Originality is hallmark of genius.

5)Genius is admirer of truth.

6)Genius just does things never argues.

7)Genius is capable of doing things what others feel impossible.

8)Genius loves to address difficulty.

9)Genius uses their emotions for execution of task at hand.

10)Genius is not born but are developed.

11)Genius believes in great works and hard work.

CHAPTER THIRTY-ONE

GREATNESS

1)Greatness is never attained by sudden flight.

2)Characteristics of greatness are generosity, humanity and moderation.

3)Greatness never comes by imitation.

4)Greatness comes not by short cuts but by using strengths. Great men are only few.

5)Great men follow simplicity.

6)Assuming responsibility makes great men.

7)Even great men also not totally perfect and they do have shortfalls.

8)Great men are truth lovers.

9)Path to greatness is lonely and very long only few people are ready to walk into it.

10)Greatness exists out of your comfort zone.

11)Greatness is more authenticity than projection.

CHAPTER THIRTY-TWO

GROWTH

1)Constant learning creates growth.

2)The difference between your worth and your desires is your growth.

3)Surest self growth is to obey and please.

4)Most people suffer from their imaginary insecurities which hold them back.

5)Natural growth is unstoppable.

6)Growth is at it's best when it is natural.

7)Being trustable gives opportunity to grow.

8)Growth is a proof of existence of life.

9)Growth is always gradual and is never instantaneous.

10)Growth is a internal adjustment to external situation.

11)You can grow only when you are out of your comfort zone.

CHAPTER THIRTY-THREE

HABIT

1)Unchecked habit converts into necessity.

2)Good habits develops when you isolate yourself from unwanted temptations.

3)The difference between good habit and bad habit is either you control the habit or habit controls you.

4)Good habit will act like a flywheel for organisation culture.

5)Bad habits resist change for good.

6)Repeatedly what is being done by you is your habit.

7)Habit reflects your unconscious mindset.

8)Habit keeps you going automatically.

9)If you repeat old habits they can't give you new results.

10)Make and follow good habits, then good habits makes your personality good.

11)When you are unsuccessful it indicates there is a necessity to switch over to new habits.

CHAPTER THIRTY-FOUR

HAPPINESS

1)People with temporary flash memory are only happy people.

2)To remain happy never think of others. Happiness makes you ignorant.

3)When you are happy others too will be happy.

4)Happiness is only transitional.

5)Happiness is highly contagious and creates positive vibrations all around.

6)Shared happiness will spread & increase multifold like rapid mutations of living cells.

7)Happiness = results – expectations.

8)Happiness is as good as your mindset.

9)Synchronised melody of Love, Work and Hope together sustains happiness throughout your life.

10)Happiness is triggered naturally.

11)Don't let your sensitivity to disturb you happiness when not required.

CHAPTER THIRTY-FIVE

HELP

1)Many give advice but few only really help.

2)Your positive attitude alone enables your superiors to support you.

3)No one is really busy, it's just your value in their priority list.

4)Never depend too much on anyone, people do change with time and circumstances.

5)Sprinkle your shine and make world beautiful.

6)Leader are there not for convincing but for helping.

7)Helping one another is natural law of existence for living beings, humans are no exception.

8)Multiple hands makes things lighter for everyone.

9)Helping each other alone achieved human progress and coexistence since ancient times.

10)You need no reason to help people. Help is done by heart not by mind.

11)Try to be a candle in life for others.

CHAPTER THIRTY-SIX

HONESTY

1)Sincere alone can recognise honesty.

2)Honesty is the first chapter of the book of education, it's a beginning of learning.

3)Honesty is never redeemed.

4)You can't make people honest just by creating rules.

5)Honest man is always treated childish. Honesty is the highest form of intimacy.

6)Honest man accepts reality as is.

7)Honesty is never profitable unless controlled.

8)You can practice honesty only in honest world.

9)Practice of honest culture saves everyones time.

10)Honesty and integrity essentials to true life.

11)Good vibes will tell you everything. Honest peoples act honesty.

CHAPTER THIRTY-SEVEN

IDEALISM

1)Idealism is too expensive to afford.

2)Idealist is more cautious than required.

3)People are mesmerised and caught by Idealism.

4)Idealism prevails when you are away from the problem.

5)Idealist are directionless.

6)Don't burn unnecessarily people with Idealism.

7)Reality can be realised by constructive rational thinking not by Idealism.

8)Idealism is just imagination and understanding of possibilities, that needn't be practicality.

9)Hardwork is required to achieve Idealism.

10)Idealism is impossible journey that you never begin.

11)Idealism is I am feasible, possible either to day or tomorrow.

CHAPTER THIRTY-EIGHT

IGNORANCE

1)Where deliberate ignorance is practiced there is no room for truth.

2)Persistent existence of ignorance can undermine existence of oneself.

3)Ignorance can't be a bliss, it's an opportunity for few to survive.

4)Ignorance can degrade organization culture.

5)Ignorance is unwanted darkness.

6)You can't ever remain ignorant.

7)Ignorance kills all human relations.

8)Direct and indirect cost of ignorance is unimaginable.

9)Being ignorant of things negatively influencing you is good.

10)Unchecked ignorance is propagating.

11)Everyone is ignorant in some or other areas.

CHAPTER THIRTY-NINE

INDIVIDUAL

1)What happens to your personal life is more important than what happening to your professional life for deciding about your professional choices.

2)Discuss your personal problems with a wise person not with everyone. Handle personal problems as a friend not as a superior.

3)Work smartly and effectively without long hours. Acts alone reflection of true personality. If you try to value everything you value nothing.

4)If you are off track you will never know where to stop. Failure is a lesson to you. Be honest with yourself.

5)We all live for desires not for achievements. People crave praise hate criticism.

6)Greatest personal gain is to respect authority. Affection knows no conscience. You can measure your real value only when you detach from self.

7)Life is equal struggle whether you fail or succeed. Never look back and regret.

8)Unless you talk to people you will never know what they will think. Human to such can make all the difference. Empathy is the boundary that separates you from others.

9)More you keep busy your mind more the tranquil time you need. Self preservation supersedes every other law.

10)Protecting your own interests in a increasingly unstable world is more important than fulfilling your own responsibilities. Those who can achieve mindfulness can only possess self control. Those who always depend on others can't take consistent positions.

11)Those who wishes to maintain a sense of integrity must accept personal responsibility for failuring to face a difficult situation.

CHAPTER FORTY

INTELLIGENCE

1)Intelligence is understanding what we learnt. Intelligence is capacity to act wisely.

2)Intelligence enables us to identify irrational means and ends.

3)Intelligence is always beautiful. Creativity is a fun of intelligence. Intelligent people just ignore irrelevant things.

4)Happiness in Intelligent people is the rarest thing.

5)Rough diamonds sometimes perceived as worthless stones by prejudice.

6)Intelligence is the capacity to remain in the present.

7)Intelligent persons never wait for opportunities they create opportunities.

8)Caution;Your emotions are capable of over powering your intelligence.

9)Our body is intelligent but not everyone intelligent.

10)Intelligence is a cleverness of adaptability to every circumstance that one encounters

11)Simultaneously both emotions and intelligence can't be at peak at same time, they are inversely related.

CHAPTER FORTY-ONE

KNOWLEDGE

1)True knowledge ignites curiosity for learning in others.

2)Anyone who stops learning is old.

3)Knowledge never makes you proud, it creates a feeling of ignorance still vast extent of yet to known by you.

4)Knowledge will become power if utilised by right person.

5)Normally we gain expertise in the field where we were not taught.

6)Knowledge is Survival.

7)Productivity is achieved by empowerment through knowledge.

8)Knowledge is new currency of modern world.

9)Mind shouldn't be filled but ignited.

10)Knowledge is meant for applying but not for display but.

11)Investment in knowledge pays future dividends.

CHAPTER FORTY-TWO

LEADERSHIP

1)You are as good as you act and lead. Help individuals to help themselves. Priorities are more important for strategy execution.

2)Forgive errors but not blunders. Never tolerate imperfections due to negligence. Force reform as and when required.

3)Improve your work areas. Do your job not others. Share new knowledge with your team. Express without inhibitions. Never hesitate to seek help when needed.

4)Accept productive and constructive opinions and critiques. Never tolerate non helping distractions. Learn to say NO as and when required.

5)Being rational is must for to be productive. Believe only in real delay justifications. If you are able to speak and act positive in a negative situation you are a real leader.

6)Set most realistic time targets & stick to them. Time is more than money. Analyse time spend. Consider only accurate facts after verifying.

7)Heart can dominate mind. Your emotions can overpower your intelligence. That is passion. Hence Accountability of leadership is a must.

8)Always look for game changing innovative ideas. Leaders have to find possible remedies to problems you can't solve on your own.

9)If you are real expert you will win authority by heart of your personnel. Good leaders fight for goals that helps everyone. Tell what remains to be done not what is done.

10)Beauty lies in leading at right moment retaining objective is a challenge for leaders. Being decisive and timely is one of the most important ability of a leader.

11)Leader should be able to see consealed risks. Leader is a pilot navigating through Strom. Leader is a person who takes us to unknown destiny through unfamiliar route.

CHAPTER FORTY-THREE

LEARNING

1)Learning imperishable. However time to time it appears in one form or another.

2)Inadequate learning can be dangerous.

3)Prerequisite for learning is one should be wise man.

4)Learning gives compassion, empathy and understanding.

5)EGO prevents from learning.

6)Life is a continuous learning either consciously or unconsciously.

7)When you accept your ignorance you are ready for learning.

8)When you stop learning w.r.t. time you are as good as uneducated.

9)Learning can't be seized from you.

10)Learning can be either slow or fast but never impossible.

11)When we stop learning we stop growing.

CHAPTER FORTY-FOUR

LETTERS

1)Use mode of letters only for non routines.

2)Use simple, clear, kind and positive words in constructive language for drafting with optimum length. Never use confusing language.

3)Each paragraph should project one point.

4)Describe negative points indirectly.

5)Body of letter should be a) introduction, b) description and discussion of the issue, c)action sought.

6)Action sought must be close ended with specified time limit.

7)Follow protocols while addressing, anyone can't write to anyone or else it will be ineffective.

8)Some times you have to write letters to generate chronological records.

9)Intra section letters must be sent through proper channel.

10)Apart from addressee letter should be marked to record keeping agency and to all relevant personnel. Addressee should be the person who is capable of addressing your issue.

11)Always present issue in a common good way to both.

CHAPTER FORTY-FIVE

LIFE

1)You will feel fulfilment and satisfaction in life when you live by values you believe in. Have the courage to choose the life of your values.

2)Try to add a new experience everyday to your life. Your life is when you think about yourself.

3)Living forward is what life actually is. Life without aim is lived with confusion.

4)Essence of life can be felt only when you live life with strengths you possess.

5)Selecting out of choices for decision is most difficult part of life having far reaching consequences.

6)If you love others they are in your heart, if you hate others they are in your mind. Fact is humans can't be without humans.

7)Helping unknown people is humanity. People who left you in a mess are the people you believe. When you live life only to please others you are likely to become mad.

8)Relationships in life are supposed to enrich you. Your relationships must make sense to you but not to others. Not everyone deserves to know real you.

9)Try to be a reason of someone's happiness not sadness. True Life is being real, humble, kind and loving.

10)Life will become beautiful when you cease to be pessimistic. When you are joyful your perceive your world joyful.

11)When you live life only to please others you are likely to become mad.

CHAPTER FORTY-SIX

LOVE

1)Partiality is a result of unconditional love and acceptance. Love is a coin with two sides as pleasure and pain.

2)More than words actions tell, how much really they care. Right one will let you know how true love feels.

3)Trust, loyalty and respect are more important in personal and professional lifes.

4)Most wonderful place to be in the world is in someone's heart. Love authentic persons not perfect persons. Perfect persons never existed.

5)Your absence won't teach them your value when your presence did not matter to them. Do not stay there where your presence being not appreciated.

6)No matter how great you are, not everybody will like you, that is life. Learn to love yourself. You are amazing just the way you are.

7)You deserve a relationship where you are celebrated instead of tolerated. Don't always express your honest opinion. Love and ego can't reside in same room.

8)Understanding is an art, not everyone is an artist. Love doesn't need to be perfect, love needs to be true. Love makes you feel stronger than ever before. People are as beautiful as they love.

9)Love is inherently invisible. Pain of love is a pulsating pain. Love exists only in loving.

10)He who loves with heart becomes inferior by dependable affinity resulting in emotional suffering. You can see your real world only when you are out of love. Love makes you vulnerable.

11)When you are in love your heart is IN and mind is OFF. Love is a synchronised harmony. You will love yourself only when others love you. Time stops in love.

CHAPTER FORTY-SEVEN

MEETING

1)Make meeting schedules predictable by fixing routine meeting schedule on fixed days except for SOS meeting.

2)Circulate meeting agenda in advance.

3)Identify purpose of meetings A)for DECISION; or B)for communication.

4)If the meeting is for decision keep participation limited to 8 persons including person for drafting minutes. If you are compelled to have meetings with more participation, organise multiple meetings at different timings or delegate other meetings.

5)If the meetings are for communication you can have more than 8 personnel participation. This is one-way participation.

6)Stick to meeting duration time schedules.

7)Only discuss points affecting more than one participants. Ask individual to individual issues to sort out seperately out of meetings.

8)Ensure all participants are attending meetings with required full preparation.

9)Issue minutes of meeting on same day by clearly indicating decisions including responsible persons for acting with time limits. Also circulate minutes to absentees and concerned persons.

10)Compile implementation status of previous meeting minutes before organising next meeting.

11)Use voice recorder and record proceedings of meetings to enable drafting of minutes.

CHAPTER FORTY-EIGHT

MINDFULNESS

1)Success depends upon your ability to perceive the present .i.e. mindfulness.

2)When you live in present every moment will be creative.

3)Mindfulness makes space, creates infinite capacity.

4)When you live in present your understanding increases and thinking disappears.

5)Mindfulness defeats prejudice.

6)You can only find solutions when you live in present.

7)Mindfulness realises your full potential.

8)Mindfulness keeps you fit and healthy.

9)Mindful people exhibit true and original personality without being hijacked by thoughts and prejudice.

10)Mindfulness makes you feel good you.

11)You will become magnetic when you live in present.

CHAPTER FORTY-NINE

MONEY

1)Nothing can be more influential than money. Money makes immediate and quick impact. Money kills most of the human problems of modern world.

2)Investing money makes you richer but not by saving money. You can make more money from money only.

3)Don't let people IN, in decisions that you can't afford. Small changes to your routine spending add upto significant savings. You can be richer by limiting your desires.

4)Normal human beings can make money only in productive age, exception is very rare due to biological limitations.

5)Money can change attitudes of people you never expected. Wealth generates envy. Money induces selfishness and irresistibly invites abuse .

6)Those who can afford today can only buy tomorrow. We are paying for our dreams. Money controls your time. Money buys you the freedom. When you are borrowing money beyond your capacity you are sabotaging your future.

7)Always think in terms of how to earn not how to spend. Disciplined will make money not smarter. Keeping money is a first step and investing wisely is second step to wealth creation.

8)Habit of expenditure remains whether you are rich or poor. Right place to store money is head not in heart. You need to forgo few crucial years of expenditure of desires for having decades of financial freedom.

9)You can't control emotions and time. Just control your money it controls your everything. If you loose money, money starts controlling you.

10)Hack of modern life is money. Cool collects. Luck and risk are twins. Winning money is never a coincidental. Not earning but managing money is the real problem for wealth creation in the modern world due to too many distractions.

11)Ability to stick around long time makes difference for investment. Laziness is poverty. Income not spend is wealth. Desire less is a drive for wealth.

CHAPTER FIFTY

MOTIVATION

1)Strong mental attitude results in greatest motivation. Motivated people are driven by passion and purpose. Those who enjoy being alone are powerful persons.

2)Good actions breed courage and confidence in others. You are motivated when you feel your goals are more important than your love.

3)Your daily routines dictate your personal and professional life's achievements. Keep your routines interesting and improving.

4)Only you can change your personal and professional life. Possess adequate energy and power to create your future.

5)When you challenge yourself it increases your ability and capacity making you to grow. Be with people who make you see the world differently.

6)Do things that are more you love. If you accept your weaknesses you are strong. Never look back; only move forward.

7)Your future begins when your fears will end. Motivation depends on your attitude.

8)Don't hold; allow yourself to grow. What breaks you makes you. Hardships and difficulties makes you best version of you.

9)Think positive talk positive feel positive do positive and get positive. Your happy when you see only good side of everything.

10)Feeling and longing are the motive forces for human creation.

11)Immense efforts and dedication without which pioneering work cannot be achieved. Stay focused; a lot can change.

CHAPTER FIFTY-ONE

OPTIMUM

1)Don't take every issue too seriously. Maintain when you can't resolve.

2)Absolute perfection is not feasible. Limit & cut short up to what is just required.

3)Addressing an issue is more important than winning an argument.

4)Accept everyone has right to disagree.

5)Acknowledge that there are upper and lower limitations everywhere.

6)Existence of optimum in reality is rare.

7)Everything has limits that make sense

8)Optimum is the only way out in a blend of coexistence.

9)Optimum is a consensus. When you optimize you will be together.

10)Optimization is a remover of constraints. It's finding opportunity in every difficulty.

11)Optimization is working better not harder.

CHAPTER FIFTY-TWO

ORDER

1)Order is law of nature. Order energize you.

2)Every disturbance must ultimately reach an equilibrium order, there is no exception.

3)If what you do is in true order you are in true direction.

4)Chaos prevails in the absence of order.

5)Order must be specific to your objectives and goals.

6)Order results in Synergy.

7)Order makes things predictable and eliminates risks.

8)Order and disorder coexist in nature.

9)Order controls your expenditure and makes your plans executable making you more productive.

10)Order enables time and schedule management.

11)Basic building blocks are random order.

CHAPTER FIFTY-THREE

PERFECTION

1)Complete adaptability is perfection. Involvement by heart makes things perfect.

2)Life doesn't demand to be perfect; It seeks to be human. Be good don't be perfect. Consistency is critical than perfection.

3)Perfectionism holds back productivity and growth. Practice makes perfect. Perfectionism is the enemy to become great. Perfectionism consumes time.

4)Perfectionism doesn't exist. It's a illusion. In reality, everyone is perfectly imperfect.

5)Once you accept your imperfections then only you can make things perfect.

6)If everything is perfect you will never learn, grow or experience. You will be bored when everything is perfect.

7)Progress is more important than perfection. Hence you need to tradeoff and optimise.

8)For some perfectionism serves as mask to procrastinate.

9)Absolute perfectionism can ever be reached. It is like chasing a mirage. No one is perfect not even close to perfect.

10)Not everyone is rich enough to bear the cost of perfectionism.

11)When your efforts are towards perfectionism you will become excellent.

CHAPTER FIFTY-FOUR

PERFORMANCE

1)You can never know performance without measuring.

2)Clarity in instructions and understanding quality will be in work.

3)Productivity can't be without performance.

4)Quality is built-in in performance.

5)Performance expectations (standards) change time to time.

6)Performance is specific to individuals as well as to circumstances.

7)Human services performance can't be measured and assessed directly.

8)Performance can be learnt.

9)Indirect cost of performance is huge.

10)Impact of performance is cascading.

11)Individual performance and performance in a team must be synchronised for Productivity.

CHAPTER FIFTY-FIVE

PERSONALITY

1)What you are willing is your personality.

2)Intellect without good character will render useless. Character only counts during critical moments.

3)Personality is like a fragrance. Personality has impression over heart.

4)Oversmart men are good but they are not the best.

5)Your professionalism depends upon degree of accommodation between theory and your personal conviction.

6)Emotional self awareness is more important for a beautiful personality.

7)Lack of empathy is due to lack of self awareness. Irrational people exhibit negativity.

8)Integrity means having self control.

9)Your personality depends upon how you treat others.

10)How you behave is more important than what you know.

11)Financial worries distinguish personalities in modern world.

CHAPTER FIFTY-SIX

PLAN

1)Vision without all facts is a mirage leads nowhere. A goal should scare less and excite more.

2)Execute with your strengths.

3)Be open to critical comments.

4)Spend less time on diagnosis more time for finding solutions.

5)Be realistic, don't waste time trying impossible targets. Accuracy of prediction depends upon the correctness of underlying theoretical assumptions.

6)Risk is risk; only continuous and continual plan iteration based on feedback can only minimise your risk. Non iteration of a plan is greatest risk.

7)Acknowledge limitations of your plan.Best and good can be never together.

8)Plan prevents confusion and optimises resources consumption. Goal is automatic order against laziness.

9)Plan is a predetermined choices for achievement. Reliability of past is a probability of future happening.

10)Think in terms of results you want to achieve for your activities. Cost of the present is future.

11)Proactive monitoring is must for timely correcting plan.

CHAPTER FIFTY-SEVEN

PROBLEM

1)Life is a succession of lessons being learnt from successes and failures. Problems are generated by 1)only thinking, thinking; 2)Not thinking. Everyone do have problems, however only some people are capable of challenging them.

2)Wisdom prevents suffering from past failures. If it is inevitable problem try to minimise your losses. Competitive spirit destroys all feelings of human fraternity and cooperation.

3)When you accept failure you will start learning for success. Never look back to history but don't repeat historical failures.

4)You can never solve problems on your own, however you can think of alternate solutions. If you are positive in a negative situation, you win.

5)Look the issue in 360 degree in every aspect. Use closed questions to reveal information. Deduce with questions till you reach answers.

6)Set time limits for realisation of the problem based on priority. Act timely as soon as possible. If problem is really important to you, you will surely find a way out.

7)Unhappy persons are the source for revealing serious problems. Never judge by others opinions. Many problems are created by our imagination.

8)If you bring unsolved problems up they treat you as if you are not doing your job. Sugar coating the past will always come back to you as problem.

9)Don't imagine answers concentrate on questions to find solutions, use previous experience of others to find solutions. Over thinking creates new problems.

10)Know which question to ask for getting right answer. Think about the answer you received but not about the person answering. Distinguish between work related problems and personal problems.

11)Before arriving at final solution you should possess complete facts. Look for the positive side in the situation. When everything is uncertain anything is possible.

CHAPTER FIFTY-EIGHT

PROCRASTINATION

1)Being disorganised is the main reason for procrastination for many.

2)Humans are designed to do only one task at any time. If you try to indulge in multitasking you will be surely forced to procrastinate.

3)Do only what you can do. Never attempt to do what you can't do else it will remain in completed.

4)Allocated tasks based on nature of task and strengths of individuals.

5)Resort to task only after complete fulfilment of prerequisites.

6)Monitor and control expensive likely procrastination tasks.

7)Do rootcause analysis of expensive and critical procrastination tasks and take corrective and preventive measures to avoid recurrence in future.

8)Ensure timely inter and intra coordination.

9)Strictly follow sequences.

10)Reach out for expert guidance whenever required.

11)Have procedures for anticipated alternatives in place in case of detour.

CHAPTER FIFTY-NINE

PRODUCTIVITY

1)Review your time spending. Is your productive time is focused on your true priorities? Care your time, time takes care of everything else.

2)Delegate all your tasks what others can do. Delegating develops confidence & ability in others. Monitor & review progress of your deligated tasks.

3)Do what you only can do by reserving specific time slot. Remember no one can do what you can only do.

4)Brush your dormant skills by refresher trainings. Without periodic short term refresher training it will be difficult to recall specific skills from subconscious mind when needed. This also helps to upgrade & keep your core competencies up-to-date.

5)Focus on tasks not on individuals. All Human bonding are emotional. When we focus on individuals we off track and we loose vision of our goals.

6)Be honest to all. Act promptly on genuine problems. Seek written accountability from responsible.

7)Productivity problems are opportunities to develop your personnel. Productivity problems triggers a feeling among all to strive for common good.

8)Feedback is a reflection of sincerity. If every feedback is positive, you have not being told whole reality.

9)Fix realistic targets. Management is a art of achieving practically objectives. Information exchange got productivity implementations.

10)Be non emotional while dealing with issues. Criticize people in private never in public.

11)Fix repeating errors and mistakes. Never accept errors without remark. Eliminate recurring problems. Don't accept NO easily. Ensuring mindful mind for all your team.

CHAPTER SIXTY

PROGRESS

1)Understand ground realities by analysing verified data. Check accuracy of facts and figures. If every feedback is positive, it may not be whole truth.

2)Faith is the battery of energy that keeps you moving beyond your capacity and ability.

3)When you lose curiosity you will stop progressing.

4)If you care present, automatically it cares future. Check daily, are we moving forward?

5)Progress is a race inbetween desires and purposes.

6)Information needs to be updated continuously for real progress.

7)Take decisions based on progress made and success achieved. Do not let one part of failure to paralyse whole.

8)Eliminate activities that are waste of time or gives endless distractions.

9)Long term progress is indirectly affected, if strategic focus is excessively on short term.

10)Progress depends upon ability to predict and control. Your future needs you, your past doesn't.

11)Progress is essential to exist. Masking truth doesn't help to progress. Others progress depends on our progress. No struggle no progress.

CHAPTER SIXTY-ONE

QUALITY

1)There is no substitute for quality. Quality is mandatory.

2)Low standard production is not productivity.

3)If you stick to standard, repetition do not occur. Strong leaders have standards.

4)Maintaining standards is a difficult job. Stick to strict standards.

5)Speed is the quality.

6)Brunout can risk quality.

7)Always look for better ways of doing things.

8)Quality reflects your commitment to excellence.

9)Training improves peoples quality skills.

10)Preaching quality & practicing quality both are not same.

11)It is really difficult to do right balance between price and quality. You have to arrive at cost of quality after estimating cost of failure.

CHAPTER SIXTY-TWO

REALITY/ TRUTH

1)Carryout open analysis when collective failure occurs.

2)Our introspection is limited to look closely at what we did.

3)Self love is normal. What you seek is within you.

4)Your world is your reality. Always find true reason.

5)We tend to seek the cause everywhere but it usually lies in our choice.

6)Without access to appropriate information your vision is blurred or blinded.

7)In a modern world of illusions it is very difficult to find the truth. Most of the facts are exaggerated and presented.

8)The day you look at yourself you are on the way of finding the truth.

9)Knowledge of truth is beautiful and wonderful.

10)Without proof you can never know the reality. Never speak truth in front of a stupid.

11)Reality looks wrong but dreams looks real.

CHAPTER SIXTY-THREE

RESOURCES

1)Segregate resources as per a)High cost; b)scarce and c) critically required.

2)Resources mentioned in distribution must be controlled by third party section.

3)Prioritise above resources distribution as per your organization objectives. All other resources can be decontrolled.

4)Resources mentioned consumption must be made as part of organisational performance indicators.

5)Resources consumption and distribution must be periodically audited internally and externally.

6)You can't treat human resources like materialistic resources.

7)Highest planning and discretion is required while allocation of human resources.

8)Plan common sharing of resources wherever feasible for Synergy.

9)Periodically review functional viability of resources for obsolescence. Replace obsolete resources in a planned way.

10)Educate your personnel about judicious use of natural resources.

11)Create a committee for planning, procurement and inventory of resources mentioned.

CHAPTER SIXTY-FOUR

RESPONSIBILITY

1)Responsibility is being honest about what you can and cannot handle.

2)Those who do not understand their assigned responsibility try to mismanage.

3)When employees morale plunge, their talent plunges.

4)Where ignorance is intentionally practiced irresponsibility flourishes.

5)Freedom is a responsibility.

6)Responsibility cannot be realised without capacity and power.

7)Your responsibility reflects your maturity.

8)It is great to responsible. Only few truly abide by their responsibility.

9)You are responsible for your life whether it is personal or professional.

10)Most people don't like to take responsibility because they always have to engage their minds not heart.

11)Be humble accept your responsibility, automatically you will find path to achieve your goals.

CHAPTER SIXTY-FIVE

REWARDS

1)Reward those who are A)TIME saving ; B)PRODUCTIVE; C)saving RESOURCES and D)does personal sacrifice for PRODUCTIVITY; E)does things for COMMON GOOD and F) preventing major CONTINGENCY.

2)Penalize those who are A)NON-PRODUCTIVE; B)IRRESPONSIBLE; C)propagating pessimistic CULTURE; D)does unjustifiable BLUNDERS.

3)Rewards can be MATERIALISTIC or NON MATERIALISTIC.

4)Be OBJECTIVE oriented and NONRATIONAL while identifying personnel for reward.

5)Loyalty is the most critical asset of the organisation. Encourage loyal personnel for voluntary academic and professional carrier development with suitable reward system.

6)When organisations productivity is economical there can't be rewards.

7)Productivity awards must be given to those who have contributed in measurement to organisation objectives common good not for individual good.

8)NON MATERIALISTIC rewards can be like additional responsibilities or job rotation or transfer to suitable location or designation or in-house training or out of housing training or awards or providing additional resources at disposal.

9)MATERIALISTIC rewards can be like promotion or cash award or tours or overtime etc.

10)Rewards can't be liberal or casual so as to lose their importance. Personnel should not take them granted.

11)Reward system should not be applied to only specific levels of organisation structure. It should be appropriately applicable at all levels.

CHAPTER SIXTY-SIX

RISK

1)Acceptance of consequences of bold achievement.

2)Opportunity and risk coexist.

3)Risk is as exiting as you think and as fearful as you feel. Risk taking depends on your attitude.

4)Biggest risk is not taking any risk under uncertainty.

5)Never risking is even risking more.

6)Progress includes taking risks as and when required.

7)No risk no miracle.

8)Challenges are hurdles in achieving goals.

9)Challenge is a risk.

10)You can resort to risk only if you can afford consequences of it's risk outcome.

11)Risk taking is like swimming in water you will be never knowing depth of water, you are dependent only on your ability to survive.

CHAPTER SIXTY-SEVEN

SELFISHNESS

1)Self care in not selfishness it is sometimes essential.

2)World is full of people with desires.

3)Most people are concerned for their own heart.

4)Good persons don't lose people but people lose you.

5)People are selfish souls with happy masks.

6)Never allow bad experiences make home in your heart.

7)You will be sorry for being real.

8)People suddenly contact you only when they benefit from you.

9)Never cry for person who does not know value of your pain.

10)Don't get too attached.

11)Be careful of your words.

CHAPTER SIXTY-EIGHT

SIMPLICITY

1)Simplicity means simplicity of heart.

2)Simplicity is a building block of nature.

3)Simplicity possess auto synchronisation.

4)If you are simple you will become abundant. Simplicity prevents procrastination.

5)Life will become lively by simplifying, simplifying.

6)Simplicity signifies peak of achievement.

7)Simplifying removes unnecessary sophistication and keeps required Priorities.

8)Simplicity appeals and looks beautiful.

9)You can achieve best answer to a problem only by simplifying.

10)Simplicity is best medicine for modern lifestyle.

11)Simplicity makes efficient and synergistic use of resources.

CHAPTER SIXTY-NINE

STRESS

1)Break, Relax and rejuvenate your mind and body.

2)Celebrate your existence i.e. daily.

3)Be optimistic & feel your life happier always.

4)Think unselfishly & view life as is.

5)You happiness nowhere it is inside you.

6)When stressed, go for counselling.

7)Good attitude converts negative stress into positive stress.

8)Workload never breaks you down, but the way you do things.

9)Your proactive reaction to stress hurts you not stress.

10)Successful are least stressed.

11)Stress is generated when you don't live in reality. Stress is a mirage; Stress is created by 99% things that you worry about never even happened.

CHAPTER SEVENTY

SUCCESS

1)Success is a decision. Success is not changing truth. Where is unity there is success.

2)Post Success only gives you free time.

3)Success is being always. Success is making measured progress in specified time.

4)Success is achieved by organising and management of things under mess.

5)Post success can attract negative habits.

6)To be successful you need to be out of your comfort zone and do what is right to do.

7)Successful never lose focus on their standards and their goals.

8)Success is a lonely traveller.

9)True success is not greed and is without expectations.

10)Humble and please can make you successful. You can travel on a road to success only when you are without negativity.

11)When you think about you not others will make you successful.

CHAPTER SEVENTY-ONE

TEAM

1)Seek team members proactive views. Get accurate team opinions and reports. If you seek advise from your team you are expected to act on it.

2)There should be healthy debate w.r.t. ideas not w.r.t. egos. Add new skills to team. Entire team must share same goals.

3)Encourage people work together as partners helping each others. For arriving consensus use open debate. Ensure team understood the aim.

4)Each team member has some value to add. Remove non performing team members. Treat everyone equal.

5)Share all relevant facts and statistics with team members for review. Never indulge in personal attack.

6)You should be tolerant of peoples differences in a team. Despite infighting you should be able to maintain.

7)Whole of our actions and desires rely on other human beings. Loyalty makes you team.

8)Your boss has to optimise between what is best for you and what is best for organisation.

9)If relationships are awkward find out root cause. Unmanaged emotions creates Conflicts. Ideal worker can be harmful to team. Normally cause friction if people do not know how to comfort the real issues.

10)Politics in a team means unspoken relationships, alliances and influence by coalitions.

11)Treat well those who are gentle, calm those who are rude, teach lessons to those who do harm.

CHAPTER SEVENTY-TWO

TIME

1)You care time, time cares your everything else. When you are unable to control your time you will be forced to accept circumstances.

2)Time is irreversible and irreplaceable.

3)Time is life whether it is personal or professional.

4)Your success depends upon how much time do you waste.

5)There is never less time only thing you don't know is how to organise the time.

6)Accurate time estimates are important.

7)Never rely on memory and do maintain time stamping log of activities.

8)You always need some quite time break for regeneration.

9)Time waits none. Your time shows what is really matters in your life.

10)If you are mindful you can never feel transition of time.

11)Analyse your time to identify effective productive hours.

CHAPTER SEVENTY-THREE

TRUST

1)You can trust personnel those with value cooperation, reliability and honesty.

2)Creating trust liberates you from control and gives you independence.

3)Trust is soul of personality.

4)Trust is like a glass, once it's broken never it's going to be same.

5)Honesty is expensive, hence few allow to practice it.

6)If you trust everyone you trust non.

7)Hardtimes reveals trust worthy ones.

8)Without trust you have nothing.

9)We trust those who don't hurt us.

10)Only few are trustworthy.

11)Becoming trustable is an emotional hijacking.

CHAPTER SEVENTY-FOUR

WELFARE

1)Work with human touch can do wonders.

2)Rational thinking and thinking with heart can't be separate.

3)Do small acts down to earth that won't cost you much to touch the hearts of your personnel.

4)Provide reasonable job security for deserved.

5)Take care of your personnel during medical emergencies.

6)Care your personnel families beyond mandatory statutory provisions.

7)Guide and impart financial education to personnel for savings as well as for investing.

8)Organise family tours to increase human to human touch and bonding.

9)Treat personnel like humans not machines.

10)Liberally provide nutritional food at subsidised price.

11)Counsel and guide your personnel if their personal problems are adversely affecting their day to day duty and functioning.

CHAPTER SEVENTY-FIVE

WISDOM

1)Wisdom makes you wise w.r.t. time.

2)Wisdom is humble.

3)Wisdom is a reflection of truth.

4)Wisdom is acquired by realised insights from life experiences.

5)Wisdom listens.

6)You will never be able to value price of wisdom.

7)Human learning for survival makes you polarised. Wisdom makes you balanced.

8)People who possess wisdom are unaffected by negativity and pessimism.

9)People with wisdom are rarer than diamonds.

10)Love and wisdom are necessities of life.

11)When you shift your personality from knowledge to wisdom you are reborn again.

Printed by Libri Plureos GmbH in Hamburg,
Germany

9 798885 464321